THE UNEXPLAINED
UFOs
AND
ALIENS

COLIN WILSON

DK PUBLISHING, INC.

A DK PUBLISHING BOOK

Project Editor *Scarlett O'Hara*
Art Editor *Sarah Ponder*
Managing Editor *Anna Kruger*
Managing Art Editor *Jacquie Gulliver*
US Editor *Camela Decaire*
Picture Research *Tom Worsley*
Production *Ruth Cobb*
DTP Designer *Nicola Studdart*
Designer *Robin Hunter*

First American Edition, 1997
4 6 8 10 9 7 5 3

Published in the United States by
DK Publishing, Inc.
95 Madison Avenue, New York, New York 10016

Visit us on the World Wide Web at http://www.dk.com

Published in Great Britain by Dorling Kindersley Limited.

Library of Congress Cataloging-in-Publication Data
UFOs and aliens.
    p.   cm. -- (The unexplained : bk. 1)
    Summary : Examines various explanations and evidence related to UFO
sightings and alien encounters throughout history.
    ISBN 0-7894-2166-6
    1. Unidentified flying objects--Sightings and encounters--Juvenile
literature. [1. Unidentified flying objects. 2. Extraterrestrial
beings.] I. Series : Unexplained (New York, NY) : bk. 1.
TL789.2.U36 1997
001.942--dc21   97-15425
                                                                   CIP
                                                                    AC

Color reproduction by G.R.B., Italy.
Printed and bound by L.E.G.O., Italy.

ACKNOWLEDGMENTS

The Publisher would like to thank: Karen Fielding for specially commissioned artwork; Nick Pope for his help with compiling the chart on p25; Terry Oakes for artworks on pp27 center right and 28 center right; and the following for their kind permission to reproduce their photographs: *(c=center; b=bottom; l=left; r=right; t=top; a=above)*

Arrow Publishers: 34tr; **Barnaby's Picture Library:** 27tl; **Corbis UK Ltd:** 28bl; **Mary Evans Picture Library:** 8bc, 10c, 11cr, 12cl, clb, 14c, tr, bc, 16clb, 22tr, cr, 23tc, 24tc, cla, 26cl, 27br, 29tl, 30bl, 32cra, 33cl, bl, br, c, 34c, 35clb, cr; **Fortean Picture Library:** 4c, 8tl, 9tl, bl, 12cr, 14cla, 15crb, 16ca, crb, 17ca, bl, bc, br, 18cr, 19cra, bl, 20clb, 21c, 22crb, 26c, clb,

27clb, cr, 29cl, cb, 30cl, 31tc, cra, cb, br, bl, 32crb, 35cla, cr, cra/ Werner Berger 20tr/ Dr G.T. Meaden 17cra/ P. Mendoza 19tc; **Galaxy Picture Library:** 36cr; **Ronald Grant Archive:** 37cb, clb, br; **Jacquie Gulliver:** 11cl, c; **Images/ The Charles Walker Collection:** 11bc, 12tc, 13tc, cb, 27clb, 32cl; **The Kobal Collection:** 6tl, 23br/ Paramount 27cla, tl; **Magnum Photos:** 36tr; **NASA:** 28cla, 37cla, borders pp8-37, endpapers; **Natural History Museum:** 25tl; **Popperfoto:** 34bl; **Quest:** 15c, 22clb, 23tr; **Science Photo Library:** B&C Alexander 21cl/ Julian Baum 36cl/ NASA 18cla, 36cb, 37tl/ NCAR 26tr/ David Nunuk 21cb/ David Parker 37c/ P. Parviainen 27br/ Robin Scagell 11tl/ Dr. S. Shostak 21crb/ F.K. Smith 27cra; **Frank Spooner Pictures:** 23cb, 34br; **Tony Stone Images:** Jeremy

Walker 18cb; **David & Michael Tarn:** 7c, 9cr, 30cr; **Telegraph Color Library:** 8bl; **US Geological Survey/ John S. Derr:** 20crb; **The Werner Forman Archive:** 10ca; **Harold Withers:** 19cr.

Jacket: **Mary Evans Picture Library:** front cl, cr, bc, back cr, tl; **Quest:** front cl; **Science Photo Library:** Dr. S. Shostak front cr, Julian Baum inside back bc; **David & Michael Tarn:** front c, inside front bc.

Every effort has been made to trace the copyright holders. DK apologizes for any unintentional omission and would be pleased, in such circumstances, to add an acknowledgment in future editions.

CONTENTS

INTRODUCTION

Fairies are carrying off a child in this drawing from 1880

My interest in UFOs and aliens began when a friend in my hometown told me she had seen one. She awoke in the middle of the night to find a bright light shining into her bedroom. Looking outside, she saw a saucer-shaped object hovering near her window. Suddenly, it rose into the air and vanished. My friend was so startled that she lay awake all night.

During the last 50 years thousands of people all over the world have had similar experiences, known as "sightings." At first, the strange objects were called "flying saucers" because they seemed to skip along like a saucer on water. Some objects turned out to be aircraft, weather balloons, or natural phenomena. Anything that could not be explained was called a UFO (Unidentified Flying Object).

Many people believe that UFOs have been visiting Earth for centuries. Some think that the goblins and little creatures of fairy tales were really visitors from outer space – in other words "aliens."

From an extraterrestrial's point of view we are the aliens...

George Adamski
interviewed on
television in 1953

Are there aliens out there?

In 1953, George Adamski from California, wrote a book about a close encounter with a being from Venus, but his story proved to be a hoax.

Many people claim that they have been "abducted" (carried off by aliens) and taken on board a UFO. Since the 1970s aliens have been described as small gray creatures with big eyes – often called "grays." Once released, the abductees sometimes forget what happened to them, although they are never hurt.

  “ He was small, like a child, with huge, dark eyes like a cat's... ”

Abductee, UK

Photograph of UFO over
São Paulo, Brazil

Hundreds of sightings and abductions are still reported every year. Some people believe that extraterrestrials plan to land on Earth one day; others think the aliens enjoy keeping us guessing...

Colin Wilson

UFOs THROUGH TIME

Although the modern "UFO craze" began with Kenneth Arnold's sighting of a flying saucer in 1947, there are many historical records that may refer to UFOs. In ancient Egypt, about 1500 BC, a "circle of fire" was reported flying through the sky. In 329 BC, Alexander the Great saw "two shining silver shields" swooping out of the clouds. Other ancient cultures, such as the Dogon of Africa and Aboriginals of Australia, have stories of visitors from space.

Spirits in the Sky

According to Aboriginal myth, the world was created by spirits called Wandjina who came to Earth in flying crafts from other worlds. When they had finished their work on Earth, the spirits left behind paintings of themselves on tree bark. There are images from many ancient cultures that seem to resemble alien astronauts.

Bark painting of a Wandjina

GREAT BALLS OF FIRE

There are many accounts of strange disks and balls appearing in the sky in medieval times. On August 7, 1566, citizens of Basel, Switzerland, woke to a very strange sight. Dozens of black globes appeared at sunrise, becoming "red and fiery" before they vanished. A similar incident occurred in 1561 in the sky over Nuremberg, Germany, when black and blood-red balls seemed to battle with gigantic red crosses.

Fiery balls over Basel, Switzerland, in 1566

" ...a very frightful spectacle... "

Eyewitness in Nuremberg, Germany, in 1561

Secret Knowledge of the Stars

Sirius has a companion star

The Dogon people of Mali, West Africa, seem to have a knowledge of astronomy that baffles scientists. In 1931, two French researchers, Marcel Griaule and Germaine Dieterlen, discovered that the Dogon know that the bright star Sirius has an invisible companion star (Sirius B) that takes 50 years to travel its egg-shaped orbit. They said this information had been given to them by space beings called the Nommo. They also believe Sirius B is very heavy. It was not until modern times that astronomers discovered Sirius B and learned that it is a white dwarf. A tiny piece of this collapsed star weighs many tons (tonnes).

Dogon cave paintings of the Nommo space gods

Rituals celebrate the gods who gave them knowledge about Sirius

" ...and fire flashing forth continually. "

Ezekiel 1:4-7

Fiery globe resembles modern descriptions of UFOs

Biblical UFO?

In about 592 BC, the biblical prophet Ezekiel explained how he saw "a great cloud with brightness around it, and fire flashing forth continually." He describes four living creatures with wings and legs. Many investigators believe Ezekiel could have been referring to an alien spacecraft and its occupants.

Ezekiel saw four creatures, each with four faces and four wings

A 15th-century woodcut of Ezekiel's vision

Sacred Sites

In Monument Valley, Utah, flat-topped rocks called mesas are sacred to the Navajo people who live there. In Navajo mythology the dramatic rock formations are the place where their gods first arrived on Earth.

Sacred mesas in Monument Valley, Utah

MESSAGES FROM SPACE

Many people think that we have been visited by beings from other planets only in recent times. The French UFO expert Jacques Vallee pointed out that many accounts of flying saucers and their occupants resemble stories of fairies and angels in ancient folklore. The Swiss writer Erich von Däniken claimed that alien astronauts had visited Earth in ancient times and helped build some of its great monuments. Evidence of more recent contact may be the appearance of complicated crop circles in fields.

Angelic Aliens
Stories about aliens have much in common with tales of angels. Angels sometimes bring messages from another world just as aliens seem to do.

Fairies from Outer Space?
Otherworldly creatures such as fairies and goblins have appeared in folklore for several centuries. There are many stories of fairies kidnapping children. In modern accounts of abductions, aliens are responsible for carrying off both children and adults.

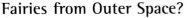

Fairies stealing a child

CROP COMMUNICATION

Crop circles were first seen in England in 1980 and now occur all over the world. The earliest examples were simple circles of flattened grain, but they have become much more complex. Crop circles such as this set (right) could not have been caused by natural means such as a whirlwind. Some people have suggested they were produced by space visitors trying to communicate with us.

Wispy Will
The will o' the wisp also appears in folk stories. He is a mischievous character that shines and floats above the ground, a little like the strange moving lights described by people nowadays as UFOs.

The Strange Theory of Erich von Däniken

In 1969, Erich von Däniken's *Chariots of the Gods* became a worldwide best-selling book. It explains von Däniken's theory that long ago Earth was visited by beings from other worlds who built such monuments as the pyramids, the Sphinx, Stonehenge, and the statues of Easter Island. He believed that these impressive structures were too massive and too complicated for early humans to have built without help. Most of von Däniken's theories have now been disproved by historians who have spent many years studying these sites.

Easter Island Heads
Von Däniken claimed "2,000 men working day and night would not be enough to carve these colossal figures..." Untrue. Explorer Thor Heyerdahl proved that a few dozen people could carve and move the statues.

The Sphinx
There is now evidence that the Sphinx of Egypt, once believed to have been built around 2500 BC, may have been built thousands of years earlier – not by space visitors, but by survivors of an older civilization.

The Pyramids of Giza
In trying to prove that the Pyramids of Giza, Egypt, could not have been built by humans, von Däniken miscalculated their weight – he multiplied it by five.

Crop circles found in Alton Barnes, Wiltshire, UK, in July 1990

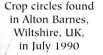

Stones were used to calculate phases of the Sun and Moon

Upright sarsen stones were hauled from the Marlborough Downs

The Great Stone Circle of Stonehenge
Von Däniken stated that Stonehenge was too advanced for people living around 3000 BC to build. We now know that its stones could have been heaved on rollers to Salisbury Plain and that its function was as a giant Sun and Moon calendar.

Are these circles created by alien beings using forces unknown to us?

FIRST SIGHTINGS

Weird and wonderful things have been seen in the sky for centuries. Many of these sightings cannot be explained. They do not appear to be secret weapons or natural phenomena – they are Unidentified Flying Objects (UFOs). In 1947, when Kenneth Arnold reported seeing objects "skipping" across the sky, the words "flying saucer" were first used. The great flying saucer craze had begun.

Kenneth Arnold

Flying Saucers

On June 24, 1947, Kenneth Arnold, from Idaho, flew a plane over the Cascade Mountains in Washington. He suddenly spotted nine V-shaped objects flying at 1,700 mph (2,735 km/h). He described the craft as "flying like a saucer would if you skipped it across water," and created the phrase "flying saucer."

Fate magazine's cover from 1948 shows Arnold's story

Drawing of an airship over Peterborough, UK, in 1909

Mystery Scareships

During 1909 there was a wave of sightings of mystery airships, or "scareships." The craft were seen in places as far apart as the UK and New Zealand. The first was seen in Peterborough, UK, on March 23, 1909. It was reported by two police officers from different parts of the city. The sightings were particularly unusual because neither Britain nor New Zealand had any airships at this time.

Foo Fighters

During World War II, American pilots reported seeing fiery lights that followed their planes. They called the lights "foo fighters" and assumed they were a secret weapon. But investigations showed that German and Japanese pilots saw them, too.

Foo fighters and a US Air Force plane in 1944

" There were 15 unidentified craft over Los Angeles... "

General Marshall

RAID ON LOS ANGELES

Mystery objects appeared in the sky over Los Angeles, California, on February 25, 1942. Searchlights picked out the craft and antiaircraft guns fired at them. The fast-moving craft did not fire back and, though they appeared to be hit, they were not damaged. The strange objects have never been identified.

Searchlights focus on objects over Los Angeles, California

UFO or Vacuum Cleaner?

This famous photograph of a fake UFO was taken by George Adamski. It is almost certainly the top of a vacuum cleaner. Adamski claimed to have made contact with aliens on several occasions. Adamski, who called himself "professor," liked to imply that he worked at the Mount Palomar Observatory in California. He actually worked in a hot dog stand at the foot of Mount Palomar.

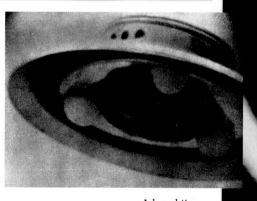

Adamski's photograph of a UFO, taken in 1952

LIGHTS AND SAUCERS

In the 1950s, UFOs were big news. There were hundreds of thousands of strange and spooky sightings reported all around the world. Dozens of books and many films were based on the phenomena. Soon everyone was watching the skies for flying saucers and mysterious lights. Many people managed to photograph what they saw. Of course, not all of these reports and photographs were genuine; some were clever hoaxes.

The weird "Lubbock lights," photographed on August 30, 1945 five days after they were first seen

THE LUBBOCK LIGHTS

Four college professors in Lubbock, Texas, were watching the sky on August 25, 1945, when they saw an amazing display of 20–30 lights forming a huge V-shape in the sky. A radar station tracked the lights and found they were traveling at 900 mph (1,450 km/h). Planes were sent out to look for the source of the lights but they failed to find anything.

Photograph of a UFO over Trindade Island

Swooping Spacecraft
A photographer on board the Brazilian naval ship *Almirante Saldhana* took four amazing photographs on January 16, 1958. They show a bizarre UFO swooping over Trindade Island in the South Atlantic. Many of the ship's crew members watched the UFO in amazement before it sped away. They described it as having a ring around it like the planet Saturn.

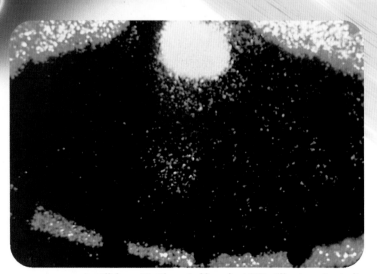

A still from Matthews's film of a UFO, Alberton, Australia

Glowing Craft
Ellis Matthews of Alberton, Australia, raced to film a strange glowing UFO he saw near his home on June 5, 1967. The film reveals a triangular craft lit by a bright white light.

A photograph taken by Gordon Falkner showing one of the Warminster UFOs

The Wonders of Warminster

The town of Warminster in Wiltshire, UK, is a place where many sightings of UFOs, strange lights, ghosts, and other unexplained happenings, have occurred. In 1965 several people reported seeing UFOs near the town. Warminster is believed to be a "window area," a special place where UFOs are often seen.

Eerie blue-green lights glowed silently overhead...

Nests of UFOs

Many people believe that ancient sites are linked by invisible lines of force known as "ley lines." These lines can be detected by some people, especially near stone circles, ancient churches, or burial mounds (barrows). Many people have seen UFOs at places where ley lines meet. Barrows have also been described as UFO "nests," places where UFOs land. Seen from above, barrows certainly look a little like flying saucers.

Barrows on Oakley Down, Dorset, UK

Are These UFOs For Real?

Model Alien

The mountains in Bernina, Italy, shown in this photograph are genuine, but the "craft" and "alien" beside it are not. They are both small models. The hoaxer was photographer Gianpetro Monguzzi, who created the photograph in July 1952.

Double Photograph

This fake photograph, taken in 1954, is made from two photographs put together. One shows four men in Taormina, Sicily, and the other shows an unusual cloud formation.

Flying Button

This photograph claimed to show a UFO flying over Venezuela. The "craft" is actually a button. The picture was produced by an airline pilot in 1963.

RECENT SIGHTINGS

Sightings of UFOs are as common today as they were 50 years ago. Witnesses from all around the world continue to report strange lights and weird craft. Recently, amazing spaceships have been spotted – some huge and complex. Sometimes craft appear over large cities though they may be witnessed by only a few people. UFOs may even have been seen by astronauts in space.

Strange Discovery
The space shuttle *Discovery* (left) shot into space in 1988. An unofficial radio operator reported hearing an interesting transmission from the shuttle. It stated that the crew had seen an alien spacecraft.

RENDLESHAM FOREST INCIDENT

One of the most important UFO sightings of the 1980s happened near a US Air Force base in Suffolk, UK. On December 27, 1980, guards went to investigate unusual lights in Rendlesham Forest, near RAF Woodbridge. They reported a glowing object hovering above the trees. A white light from the craft lit up the forest. A strange red light was also seen – it broke up into five white objects and vanished. The next day marks were found on the ground and radiation readings taken. A year later, the air force admitted the incident had taken place.

Spooky lights in Rendlesham Forest Suffolk, UK

Drawing of the
Hudson Valley UFO

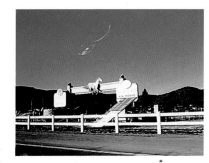

Now You See It
When Peregrine Mendoza took a picture of the Museum of the Horse, New Mexico, (left) in January 1996, the strange shape in the sky was not visible. When the film was developed, the mysterious marks in the sky appeared.

Somerset Saucer
In Somerset, UK, in 1992, Jeremy Johnson saw a "round white object" too bright and close to be a star. It vanished when he tried to photograph it. However, a saucer shape is visible in the corner of the photograph he took (right).

Ring of Lights
Between 1982 and 1987, more than 5,000 people reported seeing a UFO along the Hudson Valley in Massachusetts. The reports included sightings of triangular, circular, and boomerang-shaped objects. On June 11, 1987, a circular UFO was photographed. It was a vast black circle surrounded by a ring of colored lights.

" An enormous jet-black, silent presence... "

Michael Newell,
UFO witness

Computer artist
Harold Withers's
picture of a
UFO over
Manchester, UK

Craft in the Clouds
Mark Lloyd saw this UFO through the clouds near Manchester, UK, on January 6, 1995. He described the giant craft to a computer graphics expert who created a picture. The UFO was also seen by two airline pilots.

Bright Lights over Brazil
There are more reports of UFO sightings in Brazil than anywhere else in the world. On May 9, 1984, a huge shining object was photographed over the busy city of São Paulo, Brazil.

Photograph of glowing shape over São Paulo, Brazil

WHAT DID THEY REALLY SEE?

Of all reported sightings of UFOs, only about ten percent are accepted by investigators as genuine. Some cases are discovered to have simple explanations, such as satellites or meteors. Other sightings prove to be secret tests of new weapons or aircraft. Unusual but natural wonders such as ball lightning or the aurora borealis (northern lights) create spectacular effects. Even quite ordinary things, such as planets seen from a new angle, could be mistaken for UFOs.

Flaming Balls

Ball lightning consists of orange, yellow, or white globes the size of footballs that drift gently through windows or doors, or even walls. They can explode like a bomb. Scientists believe they are made of "plasma" – high-energy particles bound together by an electrical force.

Possible ball lightning photographed in Vorarlberg, Austria

...they looked just like flying saucers...

Lenticular clouds over Santos, Brazil

CLOUDY SAUCERS

At first glance, clouds shaped like lenses (called lenticular clouds) could be mistaken for flying saucers. However, a second look shows that the slow-moving clouds could not be spacecraft, which tend to accelerate with tremendous bursts of speed.

Photograph of "earthlights" taken during earthquake in Matsushiro, Japan

Eerie Earthlights

In some areas of the world strange yellow or white lights frequently appear near the ground. Researchers believe there is a link between movements of the Earth's crust and the appearance of these glowing globes, known as "earthlights." Construction work or earthquakes put stress on rocks and may produce this light phenomenon.

Aurora borealis
seen in
Manitoba,
Canada

Seriously Spooky Lights

Another type of earthlight known as a "spooklight" has been appearing near Marfa, Texas, for nearly 100 years. Large yellow globes, as big as basketballs, hover and dart and seem to move with purpose. The spooklights sometimes appear to encourage people to follow them but suddenly dart away if anyone gets too near. No one has yet come up with a satisfactory explanation for these "intelligent," spooky lights.

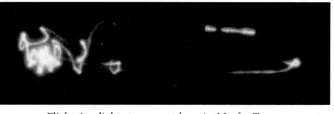

Flickering lights tease watchers in Marfa, Texas

Amazing Aurora

A breathtaking but perfectly natural light display called the aurora borealis, or northern lights, occurs near the Arctic Circle. (It is called the aurora australis or southern lights in the southern hemisphere.) This show of dancing lights is caused by charged particles from the Sun colliding with gases in Earth's atmosphere.

22,000 pieces
of junk orbit
Earth

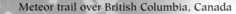

Meteor trail over British Columbia, Canada

Shooting Stars

A meteor falling rapidly through the night sky could be mistaken for a flying saucer. A meteor or shooting star is a piece of matter floating in space. If it is sucked into Earth's gravity, it becomes hot as it falls through the atmosphere and burns up before reaching Earth.

Space Junk

The space around our planet is slowly becoming a sort of junkyard. It is full of pieces of rockets and satellites that are no longer used. Occasionally, when they fall out of their orbits around Earth, these bits of debris can appear like UFOs heading for our planet.

TYPES OF CRAFT

The original "flying saucers" of the 1940s and 50s were just that – flat, circular objects, capable of incredible bursts of speed and of turning suddenly at right angles without slowing down. Often they returned to a cigar-shaped "mother ship." Later reports of UFOs show an amazing variety of sizes and shapes such as spheres and triangles in addition to saucers.

Insectlike Craft

Long, oval-shaped craft like the one above have also been reported. This shape would certainly be able to slip smoothly through the Earth's atmosphere without slowing down. The "legs" around the side of the craft may appear once it has passed through Earth's atmosphere.

CLASSIC CRAFT

This type of craft has been described by thousands of witnesses. Saucers are often able to perform maneuvers that are well beyond the capability of our jet aircraft or rockets. Recently, engineer Kenneth Behrendt from the US, figured out an antimass theory (AMT) that could explain how it is possible for a saucer to defy the force of gravity. Saucers may be powered by "cosmic rays," a form of high-energy radiation from space.

> **" We do not yet understand the aerodynamics of these craft. "**
>
> Air Force investigator

A drawing of a classic flying saucer

The Belgian Triangles

On the night of March 30, 1990, the Belgian Air Force received 2,700 reports of triangular-shaped UFOs with a bright light at each corner and sometimes a huge light in the middle. The craft appeared to hover or move very slowly, at about 25 mph (40 km/h), and then shoot off suddenly at speeds of up to 1,000 mph (1,610 km/h).

Glowing Spheres

Ball-shaped spaceships are frequently described by witnesses. Sometimes they may have an orange or yellow glow. Oval or egg-shaped craft are also common and these may be white or dark blue.

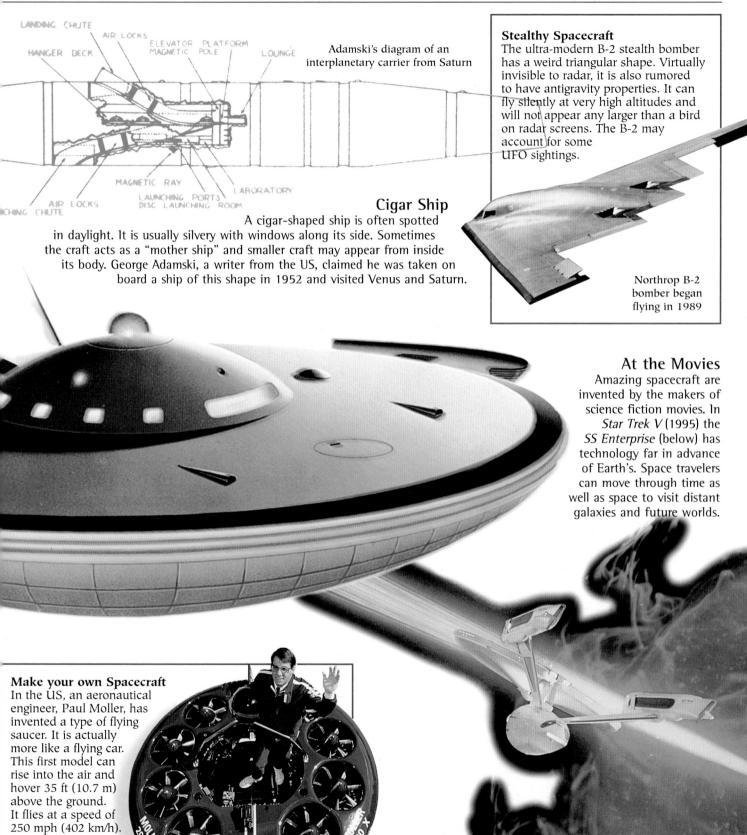

LANDING CHUTE
AIR LOCKS
HANGER DECK
ELEVATOR PLATFORM
MAGNETIC POLE
LOUNGE

Adamski's diagram of an interplanetary carrier from Saturn

MAGNETIC RAY
LAUNCHING PORTS
DISC LAUNCHING ROOM
LABORATORY
AIR LOCKS
LANDING CHUTE

Stealthy Spacecraft

The ultra-modern B-2 stealth bomber has a weird triangular shape. Virtually invisible to radar, it is also rumored to have antigravity properties. It can fly silently at very high altitudes and will not appear any larger than a bird on radar screens. The B-2 may account for some UFO sightings.

Northrop B-2 bomber began flying in 1989

Cigar Ship

A cigar-shaped ship is often spotted in daylight. It is usually silvery with windows along its side. Sometimes the craft acts as a "mother ship" and smaller craft may appear from inside its body. George Adamski, a writer from the US, claimed he was taken on board a ship of this shape in 1952 and visited Venus and Saturn.

At the Movies

Amazing spacecraft are invented by the makers of science fiction movies. In *Star Trek V* (1995) the *SS Enterprise* (below) has technology far in advance of Earth's. Space travelers can move through time as well as space to visit distant galaxies and future worlds.

Make your own Spacecraft

In the US, an aeronautical engineer, Paul Moller, has invented a type of flying saucer. It is actually more like a flying car. This first model can rise into the air and hover 35 ft (10.7 m) above the ground. It flies at a speed of 250 mph (402 km/h).

Moller's *Merlin 200 Aerobot* in 1986

UFOs AROUND THE WORLD

Reports of UFOs pour in from all over the world at the rate of thousands a year. Most accounts of sightings and abductions come from Europe, North America, Australia, South America, and Japan. Some of these countries have UFO "hot spots" – areas where most sightings occur.

Lights seen over Hessdalen

Project Hessdalen

During the 1980s strange lights of various shapes were reported performing bizarre maneuvers over the Hessdalen Valley, Norway. A team of investigators set up equipment to monitor the lights. Some experts suggest that they are some sort of "earthlights" caused by forces in the Earth's crust. The truth is that no one really knows and the investigation continues.

Recording equipment at Project Hessdalen, Norway

NORWAY

UK

EUROPE

FRANCE

SPAIN

CANARY ISLANDS

AFRICA

RUSSIAN FEDERATION

Tunguska

ASIA

CHINA

JAPAN

The northern island of Hokkaido in Japan is the site of many UFO sightings. Sightings have also occurred on Honshu Island.

In Malaysia accounts of UFO sightings date back to the 1940s. Close encounters with tiny aliens have also been reported.

MALAYSIA

Europe is a likely place to see a UFO. A great many accounts of sightings and abductions have come from France, the UK, Belgium, and Scandinavia.

SOUTH AFRICA

AUSTRALIA

KEY TO SYMBOLS USED ON MAP

	This flying saucer symbol marks places where Unidentified Flying Objects (UFOs) have been seen. Seeing a UFO is called a "sighting." Sightings of UFOs and close encounters with aliens are both indicated by this symbol.
	Sites of alien kidnappings or "abductions" are indicated by this symbol. During an abduction, a victim is taken on board a spacecraft by extraterrestrials. Sometimes the victim cannot remember exactly what happened.
	This symbol represents a hot spot. This is an area where many sightings or abductions have been reported over a period of several years. Sometimes a hot spot is called a "window area." It is not known why these sites are such good places to see a UFO.

There are reports of sightings from the African continent. Many UFOs have been seen in South Africa and on the Canary Islands off the northwestern coast of Africa.

In South Australia and the Nullarbor Plain there have been many reports of UFOs. The area around Adelaide and Melbourne is a UFO hot spot.

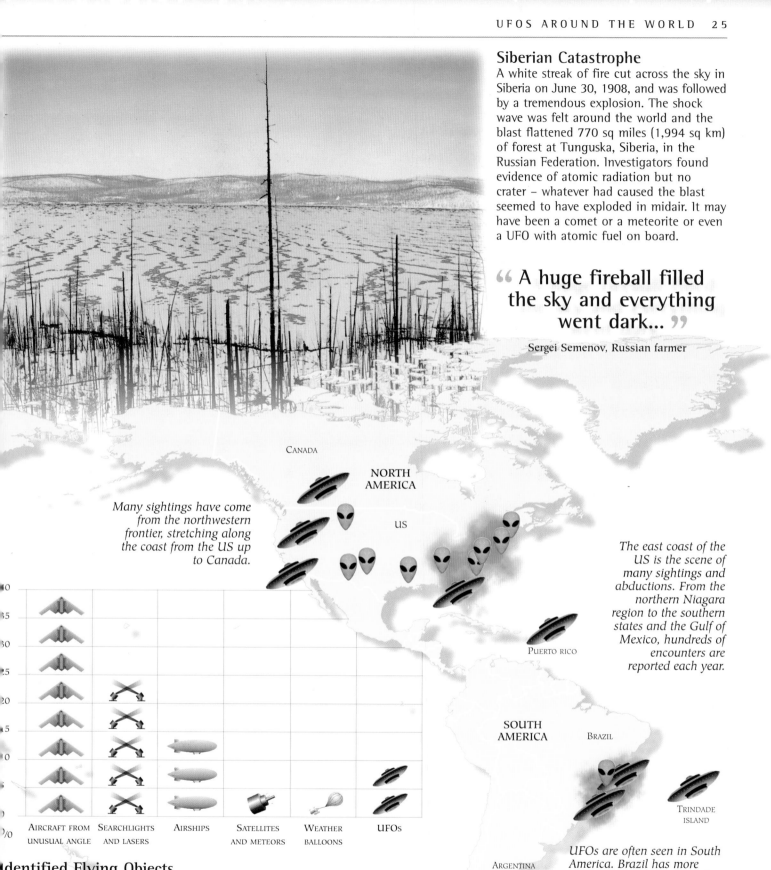

Siberian Catastrophe

A white streak of fire cut across the sky in Siberia on June 30, 1908, and was followed by a tremendous explosion. The shock wave was felt around the world and the blast flattened 770 sq miles (1,994 sq km) of forest at Tunguska, Siberia, in the Russian Federation. Investigators found evidence of atomic radiation but no crater – whatever had caused the blast seemed to have exploded in midair. It may have been a comet or a meteorite or even a UFO with atomic fuel on board.

❝ A huge fireball filled the sky and everything went dark... ❞

Sergei Semenov, Russian farmer

CANADA

NORTH AMERICA

US

Many sightings have come from the northwestern frontier, stretching along the coast from the US up to Canada.

PUERTO RICO

The east coast of the US is the scene of many sightings and abductions. From the northern Niagara region to the southern states and the Gulf of Mexico, hundreds of encounters are reported each year.

SOUTH AMERICA   BRAZIL

TRINDADE ISLAND

ARGENTINA

UFOs are often seen in South America. Brazil has more sightings than anywhere else in the world. Argentina has also been the site of reported encounters, especially near Bahia Blanca.

	AIRCRAFT FROM UNUSUAL ANGLE	SEARCHLIGHTS AND LASERS	AIRSHIPS	SATELLITES AND METEORS	WEATHER BALLOONS	UFOS
40						
35						
30						
25						
20						
15						
10						
5						
0						

Identified Flying Objects

Ufologists believe that most sightings are not reported. Of those reported about 90% can probably be explained as aircraft seen from an unusual angle or aircraft lights at night, searchlights or lasers in the sky, airships, satellites or meteors, and weather balloons. This still leaves between 5 and 10% unidentified.

CLOSE ENCOUNTERS

In the 50s and 60s reports of UFO sightings began to be replaced by "alien encounters." It seemed to investigators that extraterrestrials were trying to make contact with humans. When the first stories of alien encounters appeared, some people treated them as a joke. But others were convinced by the amazing detail of these extraordinary eyewitness accounts.

> **When I fired at it, it sounded like I'd shot into a bucket.**
>
> Elmer Sutton

Visitors from Venus

Howard Menger, from Virginia, announced in 1956 that he was in touch with friendly space people from Venus. He helped disguise the Venusians so that they looked like humans – he told the men to cut their long, blond hair. In return he received Moon potatoes.

Howard Menger, who had visited Saturn and his wife Marla, from Venus

Shy Venusian
Menger claimed this photograph shows a Venusian who did not want to reveal its face. Space probes to Venus prove that it is too hot to support life, so Menger's story must have been a hoax.

A "goblin" at Sutton Farm

THE SIEGE OF SUTTON'S FARM

On August 21, 1955, at Sutton's Farm, Hopkinsville, Kentucky, the Sutton family saw a "small shining man" approach their house. They fired a shotgun at him and he fell back, but was unhurt. The farm was suddenly surrounded by little creatures with egg-shaped heads and yellow eyes. Mr. Sutton shot at one on the roof; he floated gently to the ground and then hurried away. The police arrived but found nothing. When they left, the "goblins" returned. Everyone at the farm saw the creatures, except one person who was too scared to look.

The Martians Have Landed...

Orson Welles reading *The War of the Worlds* on the radio in 1938

On October 30, 1938, actor Orson Welles presented his own radio version of H.G. Wells's novel *The War of the Worlds*, about an invasion of Earth from Mars. He began by declaring that Martians had landed and were heading for New York. All over America, people leaped into their cars and fled. There was such panic that the radio station was forced to explain that the announcement was part of the play.

A poster advertising a movie of *The War of the Worlds*, made in 1953

Egg-shaped Encounter

In April 1964, police officer Lonnie Zamora of Socorro, New Mexico, was driving out of town when he noticed a flame in the sky and drove toward it. Suddenly, he saw a shining object that looked like a giant egg with metal legs. When Zamora approached, he saw two small creatures next to it. Then there was a great roar and the craft took off into the sky.

Landing Site
Zamora quickly radioed for help. When other police officers reached the scene, they noticed holes in the soil and some nearby bushes were still burning. The officers found four holes that could have been made by the craft's legs and five other marks that have been described as "footprints."

Dip in the ground left by the "leg" of the craft

Greenshaw's photograph of the silvery alien, taken on October 17, 1973

Silver-suited Spaceman
Police chief Jeff Greenshaw took this photograph of an "alien" near Falkville, Alabama, in 1973. The silvery alien fled and Greenshaw couldn't catch up with it in his car. Accused of being a hoaxer, chief Greenshaw later resigned.

There it Goes Again
Air force investigators could not find an explanation for what Zamora had seen. But when farmer Maurice Masse from Valensole, France, saw a picture of Zamora's craft, he was astounded. It was the same craft he had seen in his lavender fields in July 1965. He had also seen the two small creatures.

ENCOUNTERS AND CONSPIRACIES

When flying saucers were first reported, most ufologists (people who study UFOs) accepted that they were evidence of space visitors from other galaxies. Some people also believed that governments were not telling the truth about UFOs; perhaps because they thought people might panic. But, as time went by, it became clear that what was really happening was even more bizarre and frightening than anyone suspected...

Alien Space Park

When Neil Armstrong and Buzz Aldrin walked on the Moon during the 1969 *Apollo 11* mission, they may have seen an alien spacecraft. According to unofficial radio operators who listened in on the astronauts, they reported seeing a huge spaceship perched on the edge of a crater. This story was denied by NASA.

THE MEN IN BLACK

In 1953, Albert Bender of Connecticut, editor of *Space Review* magazine, was visited by three men in black suits who appeared suddenly in his bedroom. They warned Bender to close down his magazine or face serious consequences. Terrified, he obeyed their orders. Other UFO witnesses have been visited by "men in black" claiming to be government agents. But no government department will admit to their existence.

Artist's impression of
Men in Black

An investigator,
Mrs. Lewis, and
a friend look at
Snippy's body

66 **Their eyes suddenly
lit up like
flashlight bulbs...** 99

Albert Bender

Snippy Gets Snipped

Snippy, a pony belonging to Mrs. Lewis of Alamosa County, Colorado, was found dead and horribly mutilated on September 15, 1967. He had been skinned to the bone and precise cuts had been made around his neck. The body was drained of blood and some of its organs were missing. There were no footprints near the body, though oily engine marks were found on the ground. Tests could not reveal what had happened to Snippy, though several UFO sightings had been reported in that area.

Close Encounters

1 Close encounters of the first kind – seeing a UFO.

2 Close encounters of the second kind – finding physical evidence of UFOs.

3 Close encounters of the third kind – noticing aliens near a UFO.

4 Close encounters of the fourth kind – experiencing an alien abduction (a kidnapping by aliens).

5 Close encounters of the fifth kind – being contacted by aliens using signals or telepathy.

The Roswell Incident

Farmer Mac Brazel was walking in his fields near Roswell, New Mexico, on July 3, 1947, when he came across some strange, silvery wreckage. It was made from an unusual material that was very strong and springy. A short way away, Grady Barnett, an engineer, found a disk-shaped object crashed in a field. Inside and on the ground nearby were the bodies of several hairless creatures with large heads. Officials from the Roswell army base arrived at the scene and ordered everyone to leave. Later, they announced that the wreckage belonged to a crashed weather balloon.

An official with the remains of a weather balloon

Was it a Cover-up?

Roswell Base officials showed newspaper reporters the remains of a weather balloon. But Mac Brazel claimed this was not the same material he had found, which, he stated, was "like nothing made on Earth." Major Marcel, an army intelligence officer, later admitted to taking part in a cover-up.

" They were like humans but they were not humans. "

Grady Barnett

Film stills of the Roswell "alien"

Alien Examination

A film about the incident at Roswell was broadcast on television in 1995. It showed doctors examining the body of one of the creatures found at the crash site (below). According to an official, one of the creatures was found alive.

Spy Project

Experts examined the Roswell film and thought it was a hoax. Some people believe that the incident was connected with military tests. The balloon may have been part of a secret spy project.

TYPES OF ALIENS

Witnesses have reported all kinds of aliens – from green goblins to one-legged monsters. Aliens from other worlds may have developed differently than humans to suit their different environments. Many aliens are described as "humanoid," meaning that they look a little like humans. Recent encounters have been with aliens called "grays" – humanoid creatures with large heads. Filmmakers prefer aliens to be scary, but many reports show that aliens are not hostile.

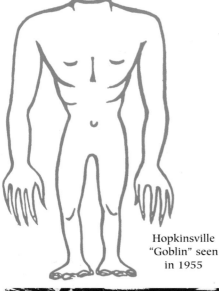

Goblin or Gremlin?
This goblinlike creature was seen in Hopkinsville, Kentucky, in 1955. It was only 34 in (87 cm) high, although its arms were 25 in (65 cm) long.

Hopkinsville "Goblin" seen in 1955

THE GRAYS

During the 1980s and 90s, many witnesses have given similar descriptions of the aliens they have encountered. They recall a small humanoid with a large head and big black eyes. This creature is known as a "gray" because it has gray skin. The gray does not appear threatening and looks a little like a child.

A typical "gray"

Monkey Business
This photograph of debris was taken on July 7, 1949 in Aztec, New Mexico. It seems to show a charred humanoid body among the wreckage. Some investigators believe the body is a monkey used in a test flight for a new aircraft. Other experts insist that the creature is still unidentified.

Body in wreckage in Aztec, New Mexico

Drawing of alien seen by Charles Hickson on October 11, 1973

What a Dummy!

This photograph appeared in a German newspaper in the 1950s. It claimed to show an alien from a UFO that had crashed near Mexico City, Mexico. The whole story was later proved to be a hoax and the "alien" was probably a dummy or even a shaved monkey.

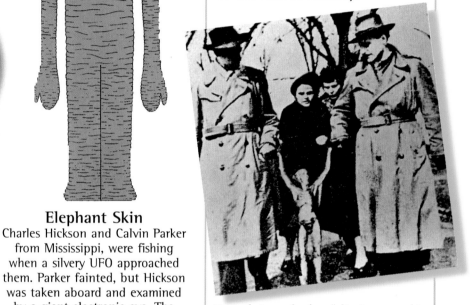

Hoax photograph of an "alien" appeared in a German newspaper on April Fools' Day

Elephant Skin

Charles Hickson and Calvin Parker from Mississippi, were fishing when a silvery UFO approached them. Parker fainted, but Hickson was taken aboard and examined by a giant electronic eye. The aliens on the craft had gray, wrinkled skin like elephants and arms with mittenlike hands.

Movie Monsters

Dalek from *Dalek – Invasion Earth*

Early science fiction movies often had incredible plots and scary aliens. In films such as *Invasion of the Hell Creatures* (1957) or *Dalek – Invasion Earth* (1966) ugly, frightening creatures plotted to take over our planet. The film *E.T.* (1977) included a close encounter with a lovable, vulnerable extraterrestrial who needed human help to get back home.

Monster from *Strange Invaders*

Weird aliens from *Invasion of the Hell Creatures*

I WAS ABDUCTED!

Until the 1960s, UFO abductions (kidnappings by aliens) were very rare. The case of Betty and Barney Hill, a couple from New Hampshire, that was abducted in 1961, was the first to become well known. Their account is similar to other abduction stories, which start with a UFO sighting. The events that follow seem to last only a few minutes but are later found to have taken several hours. Later, witnesses recall what really happened.

" Their leader told me I must forget everything. "

Betty Hill

Betty and Barney Hill

"They had gray complexions, odd-shaped heads with large craniums – getting smaller toward the chin – two slits for a nose, dark eyes, and thin blue lips."
Betty Hill's description of her abductors

MISSING TIME

Betty and Barney Hill were driving home when they passed close to a UFO. The next thing they remembered was driving away. But they realized that their journey had taken much longer than expected. Two hours were completely missing. Later, they recalled being on board the UFO for the missing time. They had been examined by aliens and then released.

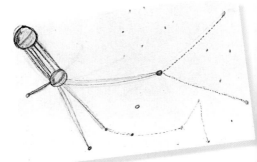

Map of the Stars
Betty Hill was shown a star map on board the spaceship. Later, she sketched what she remembered (above). The heavy lines mark alien trading routes and the dotted lines indicate expeditions. Astronomers have not been able to identify the stars.

Drawing of an alien based on Betty and Barney Hill's description

Painting of Travis Walton
caught in a beam of light

Zapped by a Beam of Light

A woodcutting crew driving near Phoenix, Arizona, on November 5, 1975, spotted a glowing UFO ahead. One man, Travis Walton, ran to the craft. His friends watched as he was sucked up into the air by a beam of light. The crew fled and Walton was missing for six days. When he reappeared, he told an amazing story. He had been taken inside the UFO and had tried to escape. He blacked out and woke to see the UFO blasting off above his head.

Have the Aliens Landed?

In a book called *Flying Saucers Have Landed* (1953), George Adamski claimed that he and six others had seen a spaceship land in the Californian desert. An alien called Orthon (pictured left) explained that the ship was from the planet Venus. Adamski described going on a trip to Venus. Modern space probes have shown that the temperature on Venus is far too hot to support life forms like ours.

> ❝ I sat there...
> looking and
> not believing
> my eyes. ❞
>
> Mike Rogers of the woodcutting crew

Burned and Blasted by a Spacecraft

On May 20, 1967, mechanic Stephen Michalak was searching for gold in a lake in Winnipeg, Canada. Suddenly he spotted two UFOs, one of which landed. Michalak waited and watched. He heard voices inside the craft and he approached and touched its surface. This was a mistake. Instantly his rubber gloves melted and his shirt burst into flames.

> ❝ It gave off waves of heat
> and the smell of sulfur. ❞
>
> Stephen Michalak

Burning Pain

Michalak suffered weight loss and sickness. The curious pattern of burns on his chest lasted for three weeks from the time he touched the bright red UFO.

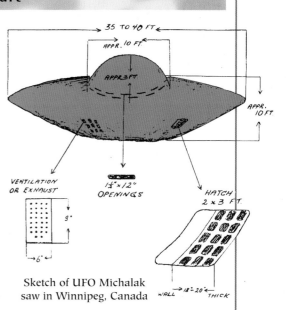

Sketch of UFO Michalak
saw in Winnipeg, Canada

35 TO 40 FT
APPR. 10 FT
APPR 3 FT
APPR. 10 FT
VENTILATION OR EXHAUST
1½" x 12" OPENINGS
HATCH 2 x 3 FT
WALL 18 – 20" THICK

SNATCHED BY ALIENS

Recently abductions have become very bizarre. Aliens have invaded the homes of witnesses. Some abductees have suffered serious physical and mental problems after an encounter. Often they are not able to remember exactly what happened. Many abductees undergo hypnosis to help them relax and recall the events.

Drawing of Antonio La Rubia and the aliens he saw

At Home with Aliens
In his book *Communion* (above), written in 1987, Whitley Strieber described his frightening encounter with aliens. His home was invaded and he felt that his mind was taken over by them.

Sickening Space Creatures
Early in the morning of September 29, 1977, bus driver Antonio La Rubia set out for work at Paciencia, near Rio de Janeiro, Brazil. Moments later he saw a blue UFO land in a field. Two robotlike creatures, each with a single leg and arms like elephants' trunks, carried him aboard. After taking a blood sample they let him go, but he felt as if his body was burning and he was sick for several days.

Waiting for the Aliens

Two hundred people wait for aliens in France, in August 1980

On November 6, 1979, at Cergy-Pontoise, France, two men claimed they saw a beam of light surround their friend's car. Their friend, Franck Fontaine, disappeared. A week later, Fontaine woke up lying in a field. Gradually, he recalled being inside a UFO. One of Fontaine's friends said he had made contact with the aliens. He arranged a meeting with them in August 1980. The aliens did not arrive. Fontaine's friend later claimed that the story had been a hoax.

Franck Fontaine

UP, UP, AND AWAY

On November 30, 1989, a car belonging to two secret service agents broke down in New York. While they were sitting in the car, they saw a woman in a nightgown float through the air and into a UFO. She had drifted out of an apartment building alongside three aliens. The woman was Linda Cortile from New York. She claimed she had been abducted many times before.

Hypnotic Experience

Linda Cortile underwent hypnosis. This helped her recall her abduction experiences. She had been kidnapped by aliens when she was a child.

Linda Cortile

" She floated through the air like an angel... "

Secret service agent

Drawing of aliens examining John Avis

Space Examination

John and Elaine Avis and their children, from Essex, UK, saw a UFO when they were driving home on October 27, 1974. They were engulfed in fog and their journey took much longer than usual. Under hypnosis, John Avis recalled entering the UFO, and being examined by 7-ft (2-m) tall aliens.

IS ANYBODY OUT THERE?

For centuries humans have wondered if they are alone in the Universe. In particular, people have looked at the Moon and our nearest planet, Mars for signs of life. The Moon is barren, but simple life forms may have been found in meteorites from Mars. Since 1971, scientists from all over the world have worked together sending out messages into deep space and listening for a reply.

Carl Jung

Fantasy World
The Swiss psychologist Carl Jung suggested that UFOs are not real. He claimed that for some people seeing a UFO is like having a dream when you believe what you are seeing is real. According to Jung, humans are searching for a deeper meaning in their lives and UFOs can give people something to believe in.

Mars Global Surveyor will begin to orbit Mars in 1997

Life on Mars?

Space probes have shown that the surface of Mars is bleak and dead. However, a Martian meteorite, discovered in Antarctica in 1984, may provide evidence that some sort of life did once exist on Mars. Under an electron microscope, tiny, tubelike "fossils" appear in the rock. The fossils are about 3.6 billion years old and may indicate that simple organisms once lived on Mars. This could mean that more complex life forms also existed there.

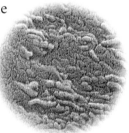

The "fossil" is a hundred times thinner than a human hair

SURVEYING THE UNIVERSE

A space probe, launched in November 1996, is on its way to Mars. It is called *Mars Global Surveyor* and it will orbit Mars in 1997 sending back detailed pictures of the surface of the planet in 1998. Probes are investigating other planets in our Solar System, such as Venus, Jupiter, and Saturn and its moons. The data they send back will give a clearer picture of our Universe, but the search for life out there has only just begun.

The meteorite from Mars found in Antarctica

Symbols on the side of the *Pioneer 10* spacecraft show aliens what we look like and where we come from

" There must be millions of other planets with life like our own. "

Carl Sagan, Astronomer

Hole at the Pole

Some ufologists believe Earth is hollow and that UFOs emerge from openings at the north and south poles. However, the "hole" shown in the photograph above is actually an area that the satellite camera could not get near enough to photograph.

Antenna with 230-ft (70-m) diameter at Goldstone Tracking Station, California

Listening to Deep Space

The Goldstone Tracking Station, in southern California, is involved in the Search for Extraterrestrial Intelligence (SETI). Radio antennae are listening for signals from outer space. Over many years it will scan the entire sky, including a thousand nearby stars like our Sun. One day it may detect signs of intelligent life.